For Ezra: You are a miracle. Keep being proud of being exactly who you are.—B.C.

For anyone who sometimes feels a bit "different," remember—it's our differences that make us who we are.—S.M.

Text and illustrations copyright © b small publishing ltd. 2023

First Sky Pony Press Edition 2023

Visit our website at skyhorsepublishing.com.

10 9 8 7 6 5 4 3 2 1

Art director: Vicky Barker   Publisher: Sam Hutchinson
Printed in China by WKT Co. Ltd. on FSC-certified paper.

Sky Pony Press books may be purchased in bulk at special discounts for sales promotions, corporate gifts, fundraising or education purposes. Special editions can also be created to specifications. For details, contact the Special Sales Department at Skyhorse Publishing, 307 West 36th Street, 11th Floor, New York, NY 10018 or info@skyhorsepublishing.com.

ISBN
978-1-5107-7509-1

ALL BODIES ARE WONDERFUL

written by inclusion & equality consultant

BETH COX

expert advice from **DEBORAH MACKAY**
Professor of Medical Epigenetics

illustrated by

SAMANTHA MEREDITH

designed by

VICKY BARKER

Sky Pony Press
New York

CONTENTS

ABOUT THIS BOOK

This book is a celebration of ALL bodies!
Read on to learn more:

. . . the incredible way every human develops.

. . . how we are all similar, yet every single person is unique.

. . . about the remarkable changes in our cells that lead to the differences between us.

. . . how each person has an impact on the world, and how the world has an impact on each person.

... how to explore who you are and to be yourself.

Because you are incredible!

Let's find out why ...

YOU ARE MADE OF STARDUST

All the elements on Earth came from the stars, which means that everything on Earth was once part of a star. That includes your body! You are made from stardust. Pretty incredible, right?

The heat inside the biggest stars is so strong it makes simple elements join together to make heavier elements.

A really big star can explode, in what is called a supernova and all the elements it made are released into space.

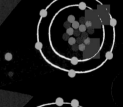

These elements combine in different ways to make new stars and things like planets and water—and some eventually made humans!

But how does this work?

An element is a substance that is made from only one type of **atom**. Atoms join together to make **molecules**.

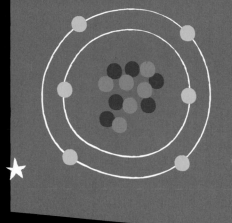

- ○ electron
- ● proton
- ○ neutron

Your body may feel solid, but it's actually made out of 7 octillion atoms floating tightly together as molecules and never quite touching! The miniscule space between them can't actually be seen, but does exist.

You lose atoms from your body as you breathe, poop, pee, and shed things like skin, boogers, and ear wax. New atoms join your body through the air you breathe, the food you eat, and what you drink.

It can be hard to believe that the atoms in you today will have once been in dinosaurs and dogs, bacteria, and trees.

The atoms making the outer layer of your skin renew every year and your skeleton every 10 years.

THE CODES THAT MADE YOU

Your body is made of 40 **trillion** cells! Inside each cell is the same library of code called DNA. This contains all the information needed to build your body and keep it working. DNA is 99.9% identical in all humans.

You were created when an egg and a sperm came together to make a single cell. They each brought one set of **genes** from the body they came from.

sperm

this cell multiplied again and again until it eventually made you

egg

the egg is 30,000 times bigger than the sperm

two sets of genes

chromosome

DNA is a very long molecule that is twisted into a **chromosome**. The DNA in the chromosome is packaged into sections called genes. A gene is an instruction for making a particular part of the body. Inside each of your cells, you have two copies of each gene—one from the egg and one from the sperm.

If you have two copies of each gene, which one does your body choose to follow? Some genes are **dominant** and some are **recessive**.

egg   sperm

D = dimples (dominant)
N = no dimples (recessive)

If the gene for having dimples is dominant and the gene for not having dimples is recessive ...

. . . . a person with one copy of each gene will end up with dimples because the dominant gene "wins!"

My moms used sperm from a donor to make me. I've got cheek dimples but neither of my moms do. This means the donor must have had cheek dimples for me to get them.

Many physical characteristics depend on more than one gene. The combination of these and whether they are dominant or recessive all play a part in who you are.

Both my parents have curly hair and I've got straight hair. These straight hair genes were in my parents, but we never knew it until they came together in me!

BEFORE YOU WERE BORN

You started life as a single cell, made from a sperm and an egg. That cell is called a **zygote** and some amazing things happen on the journey from zygote to baby!

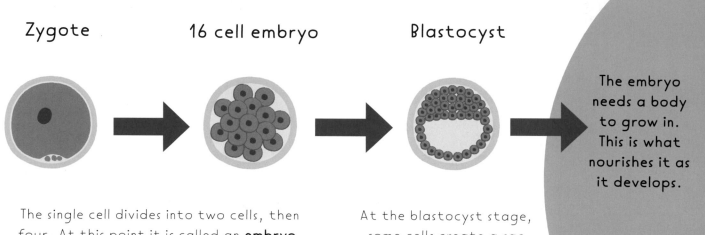

| Zygote | 16 cell embryo | Blastocyst |

The embryo needs a body to grow in. This is what nourishes it as it develops.

The single cell divides into two cells, then four. At this point it is called an **embryo**. The embryo keeps dividing over and over again to create more identical cells, each with the same set of DNA.

At the blastocyst stage, some cells create a sac around other cells that will become the baby.

If all the developing baby's cells have the same DNA, how does each cell know to grow into different body parts? Depending on where the cells are in the embryo, genes tell the cells if they will become top or bottom, left or right, or front or back of the future baby.

VOL 1   VOL 2

VOL 3   VOL 4

But how do I turn from an embryo to a human?

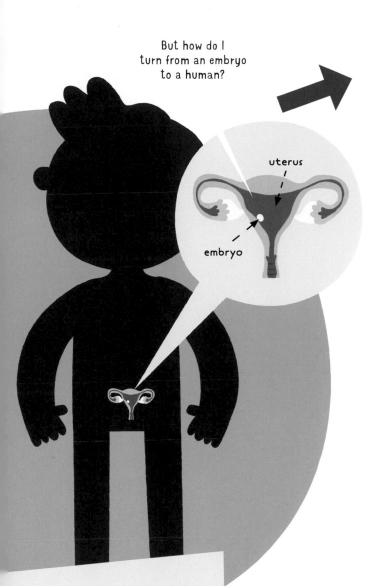

uterus

embryo

The embryo starts off as a ball and three layers start to form.

The three layers become:

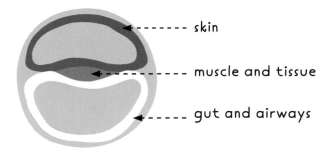

------- skin

------- muscle and tissue

------- gut and airways

When these three layers are in place, they start to fold around each other and soon the embryo begins to look something like a baby.

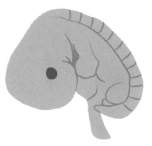

Eight weeks after the zygote was created, the embryo has developed all of the body parts and systems that a human needs. It is now called a fetus.

As the cells continue to divide and replicate, some genes are "turned" up or down, a bit like a volume control, telling each cell what to become.

As buds form that will become arms, each cell in the bud has the ability to become any part of that arm. Genes will eventually tell each cell to become part of the upper arm, elbow, lower arm, hand, finger, or even fingernail.

CHANGING GENES

Your cells are busy making copies of themselves so you can grow. Each time a cell divides in two, it has to make a copy of its DNA and as it does these changes can occur. This means your DNA ends up slightly different from your ancestors' DNA.

010101011010

Computer coding uses a code of just two numbers: 0 and 1. DNA is a code made up of four letters: A, C, G, and T. Human coding is much more complicated than computer coding . . . and we don't yet understand what all the code means!

The DNA code could change by just one letter as it's copied—and this could mean a big difference to the body or no difference at all.

Changes in the DNA code can affect how someone looks or experiences the world.

In some zygotes, an extra copy of chromosome 21 is copied into every cell of the baby's body, meaning that the baby that grows has Down's Syndrome.

Both my parents are Deaf and I am too. We all use sign language to communicate.

Ectrodactyly is when the hand is split in the middle with two fingers on each side. It can be inherited or caused by a small change when DNA is copied from cell to cell.

I'm more like my sister than different.

Deafness can also be caused by a DNA change affecting the way someone's ears work.

I have ectrodactyly but no one else in my family does.

I have a limb difference.

Signal changes in the arm bud can mean that your arm stops growing sooner than expected.

I've got one leg that is longer than the other—I wear one shoe with a thicker sole.

All these children have genetic changes that are visible. But there are many genetic changes that cannot be seen.

BEYOND YOUR DNA

Your genes contain messages that tell your body how to grow, but they aren't the whole story. There's so much in the world around us that can influence how a body grows or changes.

All these things come together naturally to create bodies that work in different ways.

When the three layers of the embryo fold around each other (see page 13) sometimes they don't join up completely around the developing spinal cord. This can lead to **spina bifida**.

That's what I have!

I've got vitiligo.

Genes can carry messages telling the immune system to destroy **pigment cells**, but that doesn't mean that everyone **genetically** related will experience the same thing.

Some genes change are passed down over thousands of generations.

Melanin is the pigment gene that determines the shade of your skin as well as how your body responds to the sun. All humans were originally from the continent of Africa and most had dark skin. As people started to migrate across the world, some developed lighter skin because these genetic changes helped them survive where there was less sun.

Africa

The sun isn't as strong in the northern hemisphere. Humans with less melanin in their bodies could absorb more vitamin D from the weak sun.

I have cerebral palsy. I use a screen to communicate.

Each person with **cerebral palsy** moves and communicates in different ways depending on how their brain talks to their body.

Humans in hotter countries needed more protection from the strong sun so having more melanin was better for them.

Now that we can wear sunscreen and take vitamins, the melanin pigment gene is not as important to survival in hot or cold climates.

BABY LABELS

In your collection of chromosomes are a pair of **sex chromosomes**. You inherited one from the sperm and one from the egg that came together to make you.

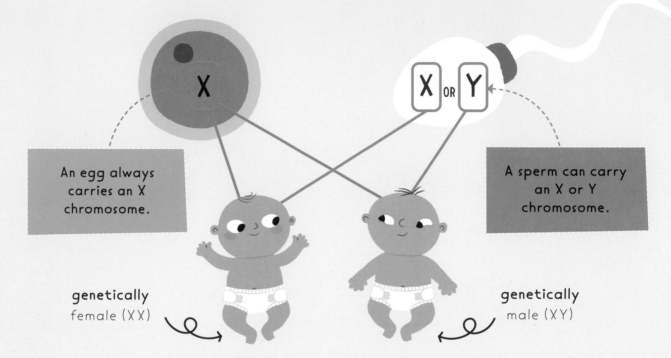

An egg always carries an X chromosome.

A sperm can carry an X or Y chromosome.

genetically female (XX)

genetically male (XY)

0-6 WEEKS → 6 WEEKS+ → 20 WEEKS

The cells that will become **genitalia** look the same in any embryo and have the potential to grow in any way.

Depending on the sex chromosome combination different genes are expressed more strongly than others, so the embryo's genitalia develop in different ways.

How a baby looks is usually used to describe their sex. This means that babies are usually labelled as either a "boy" or a "girl" at a scan or when they are born.

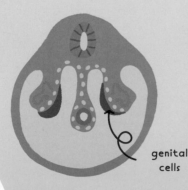

genital cells

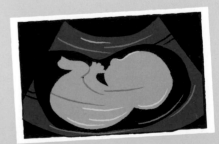

SEX

We often assume that female (XX) = girl and male (XY) = boy but that's not always the case.

You can be genetically male (XY), female (XY) or intersex.

You can feel like a girl, a boy, neither, both, or a little of one and more of the other. Read more on page 25.

GENDER

Roughly three in 200 people are intersex. This can mean that their sex chromosomes are something other than XX or XY, such as XXY. Or it can mean something changed the way the embryo understood the genes which had an impact on the way the embryo's genitalia developed.

As you can see, people do not fit neatly into two (**binary**) boxes. Sex and gender are actually **spectrums**, and people can fit anywhere on them.

GIRL   BOY

GENDER

NON-BINARY

SEX

MALE   INTERSEX   FEMALE

19

HOW THE WORLD SHAPES YOU

You are born with around 100 billion nerve cells called neurons. As you grow and learn, connections form between the neurons. The more you do something, the more connections your brain makes.

My dad speaks to me in English but Nanni and Nanna speak Gujarati. I grew up speaking both!

Living with adults who speak different languages means you are likely to learn both languages naturally.

I was adopted so although I have sporty genes from my birth mother, my mom and dad are both really musical. I've turned out more musical than athletic. I've always been good at catching things though!

What you eat and how you move, what you read, your friends, the people you live with, and the experiences you have also influence the person you become.

The way people see your **ethnicity** or **gender** can also influence the person you become. People might treat you differently or expect different things from you depending on the shade of your skin or whether they see you as a boy or a girl.

Why can't they just see me as me?

Some children are given toys based on ideas about gender.

Toys that develop nurturing skills.

Toys that strengthen spatial awareness and logic.

The sort of toys you play with as a child influences the skills you develop and the expectations you might have for the job you will do when you're older. These skills aren't controlled by your genes but by experience instead.

DISCRIMINATION

Your brain is excellent at sorting all the information it receives into categories. It helps you to organize the way you think about the world. This skill can have a downside, though, by making you judge everyone who looks similar in the same way.

THIS IS CALLED STEREOTYPING.

When people's bodies work differently, they can face barriers in everyday life.

People often think that because I am **disabled**, I can't think for myself or make my own decisions.

A lot of people are stereotyped based on their **ethnicity**. A person's ethnicity is their heritage, culture, and traditions.

People assume that because my family are Vietnamese, we only eat pho. I do love pho, but my favorite food is fish and chips!

A long time ago, European countries **colonized** other countries to try and gain more resources. The colonizers said there were different "races" of people and they (very wrongly) used skin color and facial features to categorize people and their worth.

Colonizers enslaved Black people, taking them from West Africa to other countries and treating them like objects. They made a lot of money doing this and then used this money to make their own countries more powerful.

We know that all humans are of one race—science has shown this to be true—but because many societies were built based on the false idea that skin color and behavior are linked (and because human brains like to categorize things) this idea has been kept alive.

Discrimination is when people are treated differently because of something like their ethnicity, heritage, sex, gender, or being disabled. This can be very subtle and people might not realize they are doing it. Being treated a certain way can make a difference to the opportunities you have and the person you become. People who experience things such as **racism**, **ableism**, or **sexism** have to work much harder to overcome ingrained stereotypes and prejudice.

We need to fight against the stereotypes that have been around for generations.

BEING YOURSELF

Stereotypes can stop you from exploring who you are and finding your own way to feel comfortable in your body.

Some children like to try out different clothes and hairstyles ...

... maybe because they want to challenge how people think about gender ...

... or because they feel their gender is actually different from what others think it is (see pages 16-17).

Gender expression is how you show who you are to the outside world. It doesn't have to fit with what the world expects.

Gender identity is your own sense of whether you are a boy, a girl, **non-binary** or one of many gender identities that exist.

Someone who feels their gender identity is different from what others think, might change their name, **pronouns** or how they look to help them feel happier and more comfortable.

Common pronouns
she/her/hers
he/him/his
they/them/theirs
ze/zie/hir/hirs
(See page 36.)

The hand you use to write with isn't something you decided, it's just what feels natural to you. You are allowed to use the hand that feels comfortable. Gender identity can be the same.

Someone whose gender identity is different from their assigned sex is known as **transgender**.

It's hard to be comfortable with my body when it doesn't match my gender identity.

If you don't feel comfortable in your physical body, find someone safe to talk to about how you are feeling.

INSIDE OUTSIDE

It's sometimes hard to feel comfortable when you are comparing yourself to others. But belonging isn't about your body fitting in to an idea of "normal," it's about being true to who you are . . . inside and out.

How can I belong if my body doesn't fit in?

When you try to hide or ignore something about who you are, you won't feel like you fit in.

When you are yourself, the people who matter will accept you for who you are.

Remember: no one body is better or worse than another. Learning to accept your own body will help you to think about other people's bodies with kindness.

Getting comfortable in your body can take practice.

Here are some useful things you can try.

Write down one or two things that are really great about your body. Read it every day.

I like my long hair because I can wear it in lots of different ways.

Wear the things that make you feel good, not what other people expect you to wear . . . except when you have to wear a uniform and don't have much choice.

Your body is an important part of you, but it's not all of you. What's inside, and your actions, are more important.

Belonging is a feeling. When you are being yourself, other people can feel it. It's an **instinct** that makes them want to get to know you.

27

UNIQUELY YOU

Your body is your completely unique tool for living your life. All bodies are more the same than different. Sometimes you might feel you want to magic away your differences so you can be the same as your friends, but then you wouldn't be you.

Even if you sometimes feel bad about your body, you are probably the only person thinking that way. Other people are probably thinking good things.

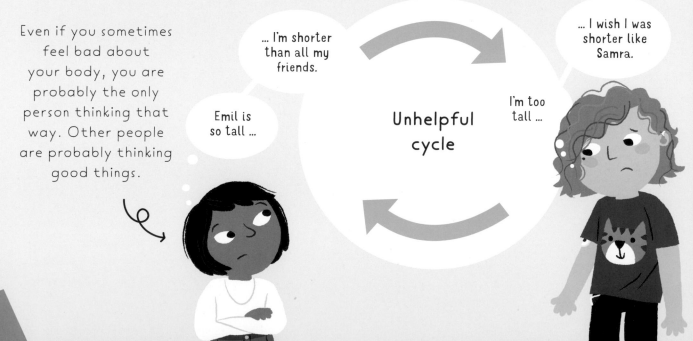

BUT WHAT IF YOU FLIPPED THINGS?

These aren't flaws...
these are unique perfections!

All my friends are different heights.

My wonky toes are interesting.

My ears make me look like me!

If you can embrace your unique perfections, you can help others embrace theirs too. Everyone can learn to look for the positives!

Let's give it a go!

I love my long fingers (they help me play piano).

I think my hair is fabulous.

This scar reminds me of learning to ride my bike. And falling off!

Assume no one is thinking negative things about you and you will stop thinking them about yourself.

Remember: every single part of you is what makes you unique. And we are all imperfectly perfect!

Be happy in yourself and your actions will reflect that.

YOUR AMAZING BODY

Bodies come in many forms, shapes, and sizes.
Every single body is as good as anyone else's.

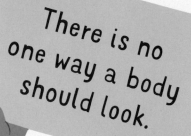

There is no one way a body should look.

But books, television, and ads often show the same types of people ...

When we are shown the same thing over and over again, our brains think that must be what is "normal."

Remember: **There is no normal and not-normal. There is just different.** And as you know from the first part of this book, differences are completely natural—it's just science!

No matter who you are, what you look like, whether you are in the minority or majority where you live, your body is different.

It's different from every single other human on the planet.

That's pretty amazing.

If we can get away from the idea of anything being "normal" life will be better for everyone!

You've only got one body so love it and look after it.

Move your body if you can
Moving your body releases happy hormones, protects your body, keeps your heart healthy, and helps you sleep better! The way you move your body is different for everyone.

Listen to your body
Your body tells you when you are hungry, when you need the toilet, when you are tired, when you are scared, and more. . .

It's important to tune in to what your body is telling you so that you can look after it.

It might be walking to school.

Or maybe dancing!

Rest your body
Sleep is when your body can heal itself and your brain can process everything from the day.

.... Z Z Z Z Z

WHAT CAN YOU DO?

You now know that all bodies are wonderful . . . but not everyone else does! What can you do about this?

It's sometimes hard to believe that one person can make a difference, but the actions of every single person add up.

Question how you think ...

When you notice your brain using a stereotype, question why and if it's correct.

Use your VOICE!

Speak up if it's safe for you to do so. If you encourage people to think differently rather than judge them, they are more likely to listen.

Some people will listen and some won't. But you might plant a seed that will grow and make them think again later on.

Listen and learn ...

You might say or do something wrong. We all do that! If you do, make sure you apologize and learn from it.

Accept difference

We are all different, and some differences might be unfamiliar to other people, or something they can't understand because they don't experience it.

GLOSSARY

Ableism
discrimination against disabled people through actions, words, assumptions, and the way the world is set up

Assigned
something that is given to someone

Atom
the tiny building blocks that make up everything in the universe

Binary
when there are only two possibilities, such as on or off

Biologically
to do with things that happen in the bodies and cells of living things

Cerebral palsy
a condition that affects the brain and how it controls muscles in the body

Chromosome
threads that organize our genes into 23 different pairs

Colonized
when one country takes control of another country, saying they own it, and enforces their way of life

Disabled
not having equal opportunities in everyday life because of a physical or social barrier

Discrimination
treating people differently based on differences, such as what they look like

Dominant
the main or more powerful thing

Embryo
something at a very early stage of its development, which in bodies means the cells that divide and grow to make a fetus

Environment
the people and places that surround a person and the events that happen there

Epigenetics
the things that control how or when the genetic code is expressed rather than the code itself

Ethnicity

a group of people who share the same culture, religion, or language

Gender

gender means "type" and has been used to group people, such as girl, boy, non-binary, or other gender identities, based on certain behaviors—these ideas can be stereotypical

Genes

packets of information that contain instructions telling our cells what to do and how to grow

Genetically

to do with our genes (see above)

Genitalia

the internal and external parts of the body that create and release eggs and sperm, grow and birth a baby, including ovaries, testes, uterus, vagina, vulva, penis

Instinct

a way of doing something that comes naturally to you and you don't have to think about it, often to do with keeping you safe

Intersex

when someone has variations from what is seen as male or female, either visible in their genitalia or less visible in their chromosomes

Neutron

one of three main parts of an atom, the neutron is the part with no electric charge

Non-binary

people who don't feel that their gender identity fits in with being a boy/man or girl/woman—they can be both, neither, or somewhere in between

Nutrients

things like vitamins and proteins in food and drink that give our body what it needs to grow and be healthy

Pigment cells

cells that make your skin the color that it is

Pronouns

short words used in place of other nouns. Personal pronouns are the words that can be used in place of your name